FROM MAPLE TREE TO SYRUP

by Melanie Mitchell

⌐ Lerner Publications Company / Minneapolis

Copyright © 2004 by Lerner Publications Company

All rights reserved. International copyright secured. No part of this book may be reproduced, stored in a retrieval system, or transmitted in any form or by any means—electronic, mechanical, photocopying, recording, or otherwise—without the prior written permission of Lerner Publications Company, except for the inclusion of brief quotations in an acknowledged review.

Lerner Publications Company
A division of Lerner Publishing Group
241 First Avenue North
Minneapolis, MN 55401 U.S.A.

Website address: www.lernerbooks.com

Library of Congress Cataloging-in-Publication Data

Mitchell, Melanie S.
  From maple tree to syrup / by Melanie Mitchell.
      p.   cm. — (Start to finish)
  Includes index.
  Summary: Briefly introduces the process by which maple syrup is made from the sap of a sugar maple tree.
  ISBN: 0–8225–1390–0 (lib. bdg. : alk. paper)
  1. Maple syrup. [1. Maple syrup.] I. Title. II. Start to finish (Minneapolis, Minn.)
  TP395.M57 2004
  664'.132—dc21   2003011735

Manufactured in the United States of America
1 2 3 4 5 6 – DP – 09 08 07 06 05 04

The photographs in this book appear courtesy of: © Todd Strand/Independent Picture Service, cover, p. 23; © Cheryl Walsh Bellville, pp. 1 (top and bottom), 7, 9, 11, 21; © Jeff Greenberg/Visuals Unlimited, p. 3; © Cornell Maple Program, p. 5; ©John Sohlden/Visuals Unlimited, p. 13; © Warren Stone/Visuals Unlimited, pp. 15, 17; © Richard Hamilton Smith/CORBIS, p. 19.

Table of Contents

Workers plant trees 4

The trees grow 6

Workers drill holes 8

Spouts are put in
the holes 10

Workers hang buckets . . . 12

The buckets are emptied . . 14

The barrels are
taken away 16

The sap is heated 18

The maple syrup
is poured 20

Time to eat! 22

Glossary 24

Index 24

Maple syrup is sweet.
How is it made?

Workers plant trees.

Maple syrup comes from sugar maple trees. Workers plant many sugar maple trees for making syrup. This group of trees is called a **sugar bush**.

The trees grow.

The sugar maple trees grow and make **sap.** Sap is a clear, sweet liquid. In early spring, the sap flows through the trees' trunk and branches. It is time to collect the sap.

Workers drill holes.

Workers drill small holes in sugar maple trees that are at least 50 years old. Only one hole is drilled in small trees. Two or three holes may be drilled in big trees.

Spouts are put in the holes.

Metal **spouts** are put into the holes in the trees. A spout is a tube that liquid can flow through.

Workers hang buckets.

Workers hang buckets on the spouts. Sap flows out of the spouts. The buckets collect the sap.

13

The buckets are emptied.

Workers empty the buckets full of sap into barrels. The buckets are put back on the spouts to collect more sap.

The barrels are taken away.

The barrels full of sap are taken to a **sugarhouse**. A sugarhouse is a place where maple syrup is made.

The sap is heated.

Workers pour the sap into long, shallow pans. The pans of sap are heated. The sap begins to boil. It becomes thick and sticky. It has turned into maple syrup!

The maple syrup is poured.

The fresh maple syrup is poured into bottles and sent to stores. People buy the syrup and take it home.

Time to eat!

It's hard to believe this sweet treat came from a tree. Try some pure maple syrup on pancakes or ice cream. Enjoy!

Glossary

sap (SAP): colorless liquid inside a tree that contains sugar

spouts (SPOWTZ): tubes that liquid flows through

sugar bush (SHU-gur BUSH): a group of sugar maple trees

sugarhouse (SHU-gur-hows): a building where maple syrup is made

Index

buying, 20

collecting, 6, 12, 14

drilling, 8

eating, 22

heating, 18

maple trees, 4, 6, 8, 10, 22

sap, 6, 12, 14, 16, 18

syrup, 4, 16, 18, 20, 22